Welcoming the New Catholic

Font and Table Series

The Font and Table Series offers pastoral perspectives on Christian baptism, confirmation and eucharist.

Other titles in the series are:

- A Catechumenate Needs Everybody: Study Guide for Parish Ministers
- At that Time: Cycles and Seasons in the Life of a Christian
- Baptism Is a Beginning
- Celebrating the Rites of Adult Initiation: Pastoral Reflections
- The Church Speaks about Sacraments with Children:
  Baptism, Confirmation, Eucharist, Penance
- Confirmation: A Parish Celebration
- Confirmed as Children, Affirmed as Teens
- Finding and Forming Sponsors and Godparents
- Guide for Sponsors
- How Does a Person Become a Catholic?
- How to Form a Catechumenate Team
- Issues in the Christian Initiation of Children
- When Should We Confirm? The Order of Initiation

Related and available through Liturgy Training Publications:

- The Rite of Christian Initiation of Adults (ritual and study editions)
- Rito de la Iniciación de Adultos (ritual and study editions)
- Catechumenate: A Journal of Christian Initiation

Third Edition

Welcoming the New Catholic
Ron Lewinski

Liturgy Training Publications

Acknowledgments

Unless otherwise noted, all references in this book are to the *Rite of Christian Initiation of Adults*, approved for use in the dioceses of the United States of America, published in 1988: © 1985, International Committee on English in the Liturgy; © 1988, United States Catholic Conference.

This book was edited by Victoria M. Tufano, with the assistance of Sarah Huck and Jennifer McGeary. It was designed by Jill Smith and typeset by Jim Mellody-Pizzato in Trump, Insignia and Helvetica. Photographs on pages 17, 21, 27 and 51 are by Antonio Pérez. Photograph on pages 83 and 87 are © 1993, Frank Casella. Photographs on pages 7, 11, 65 and 69 and the cover are © 1992, Collaborations in Communications, Inc., Florham Park, New Jersey.

Printed in the United States of America by Interstate Graphics, Inc.

ISBN 1-56854-013-2

CONTENTS

Introduction

What a soul-stirring experience it is to witness the baptism of new Christians at the Easter Vigil! As we see men and women go down into the waters of baptism, the words of St. Paul echo in our ears: "Are you not aware that we who were baptized into Christ Jesus were baptized into his death?" (Romans 6:3 – 4) When new Christians emerge from the baptismal waters, we know that God has claimed them as sons and daughters. They have been freed of sin; they need not fear death.

This awesome celebration is the culmination of a long process of formation for the catechumens. They will have spent a year or longer in preparation for this night. They will have listened to the word of God, learned to pray, become immersed in the tradition of the church, received the counsel of sponsors and catechists, and begun to enter into apostolic service. From many members of the parish community they will have learned what it means to live the life of a baptized Catholic.

Underlying all this preparation is the call to conversion. Without a conversion of mind and heart there would be little to celebrate. The call to conversion is the call to turn away from whatever is contrary to the gospel. To be converted is to trust in God as the source of all life and hope.

The ministry of preparing men and women for the sacraments of Christian initiation — a ministry that belongs to the entire Christian community — is both joyful and challenging. It is joyful because we can experience the presence of the Holy Spirit among us as we witness the change and growth in another's faith. It is challenging because we become aware of our own need for conversion as we call others to it.

If we accept this challenge, the Easter Vigil becomes a celebration for us as much as for the newly baptized. We stand with the catechumens at the font of baptism. We proclaim with renewed conviction, "I do believe." We pledge once again to live as members of Christ's body. We recognize that the church is always in need of deeper conversion.

How Do We Welcome New Catholics?

The church has provided a process for Christian initiation that follows a progression that is the fruit of hundreds of years of wisdom and experience. The *Rite of Christian Initiation of Adults* is a plan for the way Catholics welcome and form adults and children of catechetical age in the way of Jesus as it is lived in the Catholic tradition. While it is a ritual book, it contains much more than prayers and rubrics. It offers a vision of what it means to be converted and to live for Christ in the church. It presents a series of steps and stages, each with its own distinctive expectations for learning, praying, personal change and spiritual growth. The *Rite of Christian Initiation of Adults* is a call to the Catholic community to see itself as a welcoming and initiating community. The rite invites the local community to be the nucleus within which and through which the formation of new members takes place.

When some people first hold a copy of the *Rite of Christian Initiation of Adults* in their hands they are overwhelmed — so many pages, so many words, so many rituals. The rite lays out an ideal plan for ministering to adults from the time they first inquire about the faith to the time of their baptism. At first, some people feel the church's plan of initiation is unrealistic or burdensome because of its complex structure and the time that is presumed for the whole initiation process. Those who have been active in the ministry of initiation for a number of years are quick to report that what at first may appear to be a long process actually passes quickly. It frequently feels like there wasn't enough time to do everything well.

One of the reasons the *Rite of Christian Initiation of Adults* is so extensive is that it provides several options for a variety of circumstances. There are options to be used for an unbaptized adult, for children of catechetical age, for men and women who are baptized but who were never formed in the traditions and teachings of the faith, for baptized Catholics who seek to complete their initiation by being confirmed or receiving the eucharist or both, and for baptized Christians from other churches who are preparing to be received into the full communion of the Roman Catholic church. Each of these different groups of people require particular attention and a process tailored to their needs.

Since the present *Rite of Christian Initiation of Adults* was published in English in 1974, parish communities around the world have found the plan, or order, of initiation most helpful in welcoming new Catholics. Parish ministers often tell how they began very simply by implementing what they could, and then year by year built on their earlier efforts. Many have testified how effective this process of initiation has been for the renewal of the whole parish.

This book is intended for anyone who would like to understand the purpose, basic order and dynamic of Christian initiation as it is found in the *Rite of Christian Initiation of Adults.* If possible, read this book with a copy of the *Rite of Christian Initiation of Adults* nearby; frequent reference will be made to paragraphs in the rite.

As you begin to study this book, keep in mind that the *Rite of Christian Initiation of Adults* is not a manual for welcoming new Catholics or a prepackaged program that includes everything needed to welcome inquirers, counsel, catechize and pray. The purpose of *Welcoming the New Catholic* is to help you understand the spirit of the rite, its components, its assumptions and its language.

One of the key principles for understanding the process of Christian initiation is *flexibility.* While there are norms to be followed, welcoming new Catholics is primarily a matter of pastoral care. Not everyone who seeks the sacraments of initiation needs to undergo the same preparation as everyone else, and it would be a grave mistake to try to force them to. Each person should be given what he or she needs.

Since the first edition of *Welcoming the New Catholic* was published in 1978, the *Rite of Christian Initiation of Adults* has itself been revised to include a number of adaptations for the Catholic church in the United States. This new edition of *Welcoming the New Catholic* reflects those changes as well as other changes in pastoral approach that have been born from pastoral experience in Christian initiation over the last two decades.

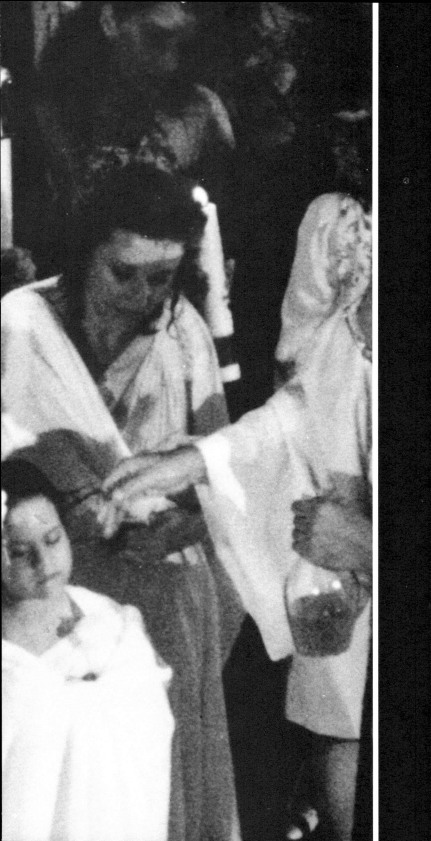

Christian Initiation:

Pastoral Principles

Before we examine the various stages and periods of the order of Christian initiation, it will be helpful to examine some of the principles on which initiation works.

Initiation Takes Place in Community

To say that the process of initiation takes place in community does not simply mean that the liturgical rites are celebrated in the community. It means that the community is an essential element of the formation of new numbers. By its witness and its words, the community passes on its values and beliefs.

The quality and depth of a parish's communal life has a great bearing on the formation of new members. Candidates (baptized persons preparing to be received into the Catholic church) and catechumens (unbaptized persons preparing for Christian initiation) learn to pray as they experience the prayer of the community. They learn to serve as they see others serve.

They can be moved to accept as their own the values and teachings of Jesus as they encounter Catholics who live these values and teachings with conviction.

In a large community it is difficult to expect everyone to have close contact with the inquirers (persons who are seeking to learn more about the Catholic church), candidates and catechumens. For this reason a catechumenal community is formed, consisting of catechists, sponsors, pastors and others who represent the larger church community in ministering to the inquirers, candidates and catechumens. These ministries will be discussed more completely in chapter four.

The value of this principle of community is that it clearly reminds us that it is a *living faith* into which we are welcoming new members. We are not initiating people into a catechism or some theoretical idea of what church is. We are initiating new members into a flesh-and-blood body of believers who live the Catholic tradition and who have found meaning for their lives in that tradition.

Without an understanding of the basic principle that initiation is communal, one might think that learning the Catholic catechism is all that is necessary to be a Catholic. Or one might conclude that to be a person of faith is a private affair between oneself and God.

Catholics believe that Christ is inseparable from his church. Consequently our initiation into Christ also means initiation into the living church. To live the Catholic faith is to live by faith in the church. If the full effect of initiation is to be realized, the community's involvement in the process of Christian initiation is of paramount importance.

Conversion Is the Heart of Initiation

Conversion is not just a matter of believing in God, Jesus and the Holy Spirit. Conversion also means accepting what Jesus taught, interiorizing the values and teachings of Jesus. Conversion is not just an intellectual act but a change in the way life is lived. Because conversion involves a change in mind and heart, it can be a gut-wrenching struggle to reshape one's way of thinking, priorities, relationships and style of life. While conversion is a very personal experience, it cannot become a mere private affair. Conversion leads us into the world where we live our faith. Conversion compels us to further the mission of Jesus to transform the world into the kingdom of God.

In the process of conversion, one comes to experience more deeply the immense love and mercy of God so freely given. This, in turn, often engenders a feeling of unworthiness and sinfulness that calls for healing and forgiveness. Repentance often is a part of conversion.

Each of us knows that the process of conversion is not finished in our own lives. This helps us to be respectful and realistic about our expectations of others. Because the process of conversion involves the whole of a person's life, we cannot program conversion into a fixed time. Each individual moved by God's grace will journey along the path of conversion at his or her own pace. This process usually will take place gradually over a long period of time.

More will be said about conversion in chapter three.

Initiation Includes Liturgical Rites

While the sacraments of baptism, confirmation and eucharist are the climax of the initiation process, there are several other

ritual experiences that punctuate an individual's growth in faith. The order of initiation includes the rite of acceptance into the order of catechumens, the rite of election, blessings, scrutinies and liturgies of the word. The U.S. edition of the *Rite of Christian Initiation of Adults* also includes a number of optional rites for baptized candidates. These include the rite of welcoming, the call to continuing conversion and a penitential rite.

These various rituals not only mark and celebrate progression in faith but, like all liturgical experiences, they also have the power to convey what words alone cannot. Ritual not only gives form to our prayer, it shapes our attitudes and values as well. Ritual has the power to draw us beyond ourselves into the mystery of God who transforms us.

The liturgical rites in the order of initiation, then, are not optional prayer services, mere addenda to the initiation process. These rites are part of the church's worship life. They involve the entire community, and they poignantly remind us that God is among us working to save us.

Initiation Includes Catechesis

Faith is a gift. But that faith needs to be enlightened. The church's rich tradition of teaching is an invaluable asset. Over many centuries the church has reflected on the meaning of life and death, the revelation of the true God, moral choices, biblical truths, worship, sin and grace, and so much more. The teachings of the church, including its formal doctrines and creeds, help us to make sense out of our existence as we reflect on the implications of faith. During the period of the catechumenate, this catechetical component of the initiation process is most evident.

The *Rite of Christian Initiation of Adults* notes that a thorough catechesis should be accommodated to the liturgical year (75). The liturgical year, or the church's calendar, is a yearlong celebration of the mystery of Christ. From season to season we are drawn into the life, death, resurrection and exaltation of Christ. This unfolding of the mystery of Christ is not a historical review but a gradual remaking of our own lives as we reflect on the mysteries we celebrate.

Each feast and season has its own character, its own message, its own special grace. By integrating the catechesis of new Catholics within the liturgical year, our teaching is reinforced by the feasts and seasons we celebrate. A solid catechesis on the importance of turning away from sin, for example, is effectively reinforced by the rhythm and discipline of Lent. Our catechesis on the incarnation is supported and taken to a deeper level when we observe the Christmas Season.

As the candidates walk through the entire year with the community, they learn to make the church's rhythm of life their own and to discover how the liturgical calendar of feasts and seasons can be an ongoing source of spiritual growth and enlightenment.

Initiation Means Mission

The process of Christian initiation ultimately leads to mission. While the celebration of baptism, confirmation and eucharist is the climactic point in becoming a Catholic, it is not the end of the journey. Becoming a Christian means accepting a share in the mission of Jesus. We are not adopted by God to live apart from the world, as if faith were a private possession. Faith and baptism are highly personal, but they are directed outward.

13

Jesus' mission was to proclaim the reign of God. He came among us to transform the world into a kingdom of truth, grace, holiness, love, justice and peace. When we are baptized into Christ Jesus we inherit the mission that Jesus entrusted to his church.

In the process of Christian formation that leads to the initiation sacraments, the church is charged with the responsibility of preparing new members for active discipleship. Everyone is blessed with different gifts. Parish catechumenate ministers are called to help each catechumen or candidate discern his or her gifts and to support the use of those gifts for the life of the world.

We are not preparing Christians to live their lives in the church sacristy but in the world of work and family, a society of trade and commerce, a world filled with many conflicting values, both good and evil. To live one's faith in the world, one must be prepared to face the world and to do one's part in the transformation of society into the kingdom of God.

By a gradual introduction to the works of service in the parish community and beyond, and by a suitable apprenticeship in the Christian community, candidates will gradually learn to make the mission of Jesus an important dimension of their life.

Initiation Demands Adaptability

There is a temptation to try to create one structured and well-ordered process that will accommodate every potential new member of the church. While doing so might make the work easier and provide a plan that looks tidy on paper, it is not realistic. Welcoming new Catholics is not a program but a ministry to men, women and children who seek the Lord and desire to live in faith with the Catholic community. Each one served will be unique, so those who work in the ministry of initiation must be adaptable.

Pastoral adaptability presumes a flexibility that sometimes may look or feel messy. Initiation ministers need to learn to be comfortable with this messiness and not try to put order into something that by its very nature is going to be varied and at times unpredictable. This, however, does not negate the need for preparation and planning. What it does mean is that even after all the planning has taken place, we must be ready to redesign what we planned when the needs of the catechumens and candidates suggest another direction.

Pastoral adaptability does not mean, however, that we may create our own rites or disregard the process of initiation outlined in the *Rite of Christian Initiation of Adults*. Any form of adaptation needs to grow from what already is given.

CHAPTER TWO

For Whom Is This Rite Intended?

Paragraph one of the *Rite of Christian Initiation of Adults* tells us:

> The rite of Christian initiation presented here is designed for adults who, after hearing the mystery of Christ proclaimed, consciously and freely seek the living God and enter the way of faith and conversion as the Holy Spirit opens their hearts.

This description of who might be included in the initiation process allows for a wide range of potential candidates. There will be a variety of circumstances that may lead individuals to inquire about becoming Catholic. Some will have very little formal religious background; others may have been given a Christian upbringing as a child. Although people in various circumstances must be treated according to their own needs and situations, the *Rite of Christian Initiation of Adults* provides a framework for ministering to many, although not all, people. What follows is an overview of the general categories of persons we might expect to find in our ministry of Christian initiation.

Unbaptized Adults

Some of the people who seek to join the Catholic church will be unbaptized and have little or no religious upbringing or knowledge. Part I of the *Rite of Christian Initiation of Adults* (1–251) is the complete form of the order of initiation that is used in ministering to unbaptized persons. Part I outlines how the church serves individuals from their first inquiry through the time following the celebration of the sacraments of initiation.

It may be that some of the unbaptized persons who come to us will be quite religious, acquainted with the scriptures and in the habit of regular prayer. Although the complete form of the order of initiation as found in Part I would be followed, sensitivity to the individual's experience and needs will necessitate some accommodation, including the extent of the catechetical formation a person may need.

Unbaptized Children

Although the book describing the initiation process is titled *Rite of Christian Initiation of Adults*, it also is intended for unbaptized children who have reached catechetical age (approximately seven years old). Part II, chapter 1 (252–330) takes the basic order of initiation found in Part I and adapts it for children. What is distinctive in this chapter is the pastoral concern for including the parents and the children's peer group in the initiation process.

The rite presumes that there will be a wide range of ages and levels of maturity among the children. Nevertheless, their formation, like that for the adults, is directed to fostering a conversion of mind and heart at the level they are capable of and on their initiation into the mystery of Christ and the church. This is not the same focus as religious education, which, it is hoped, will continue throughout the child's life and build on the formation given in the initiation process.

Baptized but Uncatechized Adults Preparing for Reception into the Full Communion of the Catholic Church

People who are baptized but were never catechized and who now wish to be received into the full communion of the Catholic church are frequently encountered in parish catechumenates. These individuals may have been baptized in other churches in the Christian tradition, for example, Methodist, Lutheran, Baptist or Disciples of Christ, but they may not have not had much or any religious formation. They usually are believers, but not active in any church. Quite often they are married to a Catholic.

Part II, chapter 4 ("Preparation of Uncatechized Adults for Confirmation and Eucharist," 400–472) of the *Rite of Christian Initiation of Adults* can be used with Part II, chapter 5 ("Reception of Baptized Christians into the Full Communion of the Catholic Church," 473–504) in ministering to these individuals.

The church urges us to be very sensitive in our ministry to the baptized. We should not impose more on these individuals than is necessary, and we must respect the baptismal status of these candidates. By virtue of the one baptism they are already claimed by Christ and joined to the church, although incompletely joined to the Roman Catholic church.

While church law requires very little of individuals being received into the full communion of the Catholic church, pastoral experience demonstrates that many who are baptized

have not been evangelized or catechized. They may be familiar with some basic Christian truths and biblical stories, but the baptism each received as a child may not have had an opportunity to bear fruit in a living faith. These individuals, referred to as *candidates,* may well need the same spiritual and catechetical formation as the unbaptized.

The edition of the *Rite of Christian Initiation of Adults* for the dioceses of the United States provides a set of rites for baptized candidates. These parallel the rites used with the unbaptized and can be invaluable in drawing the candidates more deeply into Christ and stirring up within them the grace of their baptism.

It is not uncommon to welcome someone who was baptized Christian, was raised in a religious family and is well catechized. It would be inappropriate for such an individual to be expected to participate in the complete initiation process intended for the unbaptized. All that may be necessary is pastoral counsel, an introduction to the community and its life, participation in prayer, limited catechesis, and guidance into the church's apostolic life—all tailored to the individual's needs and respectful of the gifts each one brings.

Children of catechetical age also may be included in this category. Their formation will need to be accommodated to their level of maturity.

In ministering to baptized persons preparing for reception into full communion, we can err by demanding either too much or too little. Through individual pastoral interviews, ministers can ascertain the needs and levels of faith which in turn will give direction to how we shape our ministry to the candidates.

Uncatechized Adults Preparing for Confirmation and Eucharist

There are individuals who were baptized Catholic but never were confirmed and never have received the eucharist. Most frequently these individuals are uncatechized. Ordinarily they share a great deal in common with the baptized, uncatechized people preparing for reception into the Catholic church. Like them, uncatechized Catholics often need a fresh evangelization that calls them to a converted life. They need a thorough catechesis and a solid foundation on which they can continue to build their Christian lives. They need the opportunity to stir up the grace of their baptism.

Part II, chapter 4 ("Preparation of Uncatechized Adults for Confirmation and Eucharist," 400–472) is suited for these individuals. Other parts of the *Rite of Christian Initiation of Adults* can also be adapted and used in ministering to these individuals to the extent that these components are appropriate and do not impose pragmatic elements that are not helpful.

Individuals in Exceptional Circumstances

There will be times when, because of illness or age or an impending move, the complete order of initiation may not be possible. Part II, chapter 2 ("Christian Initiation of Adults in Exceptional Circumstances," 331–369) may be used in these situations. The order of initiation also provides for a person in danger of death, whether unbaptized or baptized. Part II, chapter 3 ("Christian Initiation of a Person in Danger of Death," 370–399) is used in these pastoral situations.

What the *Rite of Christian Initiation of Adults* tries to establish is that even in exceptional circumstances, some of what we experience in the complete order should be used to whatever extent is possible. These provisions for exceptional circumstances should not be interpreted as shortcuts for the convenience of the ministers.

Persons Baptized in an Eastern Catholic Church or an Orthodox Church

When individuals who were baptized in an Eastern Catholic church or an Orthodox church seek to be admitted into the Roman Catholic church, they cannot be formally received into the Latin (Roman) rite of the Catholic church without first receiving the appropriate permission to transfer rites. An Orthodox Christian usually is to be received into the corresponding Eastern Catholic church (for example, a Greek Orthodox Christian would be received into the Melkite Catholic church, and a Ukrainian Orthodox Christian would be received into the Ukrainian Catholic church). Because of the complex and sensitive ecumenical nature of these cases, parish ministers should consult with their chancery as soon as a situation such as this presents itself.

Once the necessary permissions have been obtained to transfer rites, an individual can be included in the group of candidates preparing for reception into the full communion of the Catholic church.

Catholics Returning to the Church

While there may be many similarities between unbaptized inquirers or candidates preparing for reception into the Catholic church and a returning Catholic, placing the returning Catholic in the group with all the others is not recommended. The experience of returning Catholics may diffuse the focus and disrupt the dynamic of initial faith and exploration of Catholic life, teaching and worship that is geared to those first joining the church.

Methods such as those used with catechumens and candidates can be valuable. Returning Catholics, however, deserve their own process of healing, reconciliation, catechesis and reintegration into Catholic life. For these individuals, parish ministry leads them to the sacrament of penance and the celebration of the eucharist.

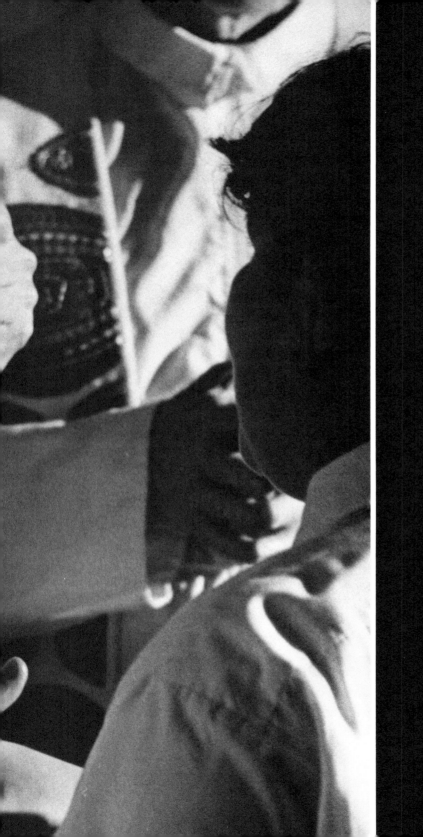

CHAPTER THREE

A Structure for the Christian Initiation of Adults

There are four distinct periods described in the *Rite of Christian Initiation of Adults* that mark the spiritual journey of adults:

- precatechumenate, or period of evangelization
- catechumenate
- period of purification and enlightenment (Lent)
- period of postbaptismal catechesis or mystagogy (Easter–Pentecost)

The rite also describes three "stages," or rituals, that mark the transition from one period to the next. Each stage for unbaptized persons has a parallel for baptized candidates (the stage for baptized candidates appears in parentheses):

- Rite of Acceptance into the Order of Catechumens, 41–74 (Rite of Welcoming the Candidates, 411–433)
- Rite of Election or Enrollment of Names, 118–137 (Rite of Calling the Candidates to Continuing Conversion, 446–458)
- Celebration of the Sacraments of Initiation, 206–243 (Reception of Baptized Christians into the Full Communion of the Catholic Church, 473–504, or Celebration

at the Easter Vigil of the Sacraments of Initiation and of the Rite of Reception into the Full Communion of the Catholic Church, 562–594)

These liturgical rites flow naturally from the spiritual formation and catechesis that is offered to prospective new Catholics. The liturgical rites are integral to the whole process of conversion and initiation.

While these periods and stages provide an order for the initiation process, they do not constitute a recipe or guaranteed formula for initiation. One must constantly be reminded that it is our personal investment in the periods and stages that gives life to the process. And it is the action of the Holy Spirit that makes the conversion process effective. The rest of this chapter presents a brief overview of each of the periods and stages.

Precatechumenate

The first period is called evangelization, or precatechumenate. This is a time when "the living God is proclaimed and Jesus Christ whom he has sent for the salvation of all. Thus those who are not yet Christians, their hearts opened by the Holy Spirit, may believe and be freely converted to the Lord" (36). It is at this point that the church most opportunely exercises its vocation as evangelizer. Pope Paul VI reminded us of the church's call to evangelize, a role clearly exercised in the initiation of new members:

> It is above all Jesus' mission and his condition of being an evangelizer that the church is called upon to continue. For the Christian community is never closed in upon itself. The intimate life of this community—the life of listening to the word, and the sharing of bread—this intimate life

> only acquires its full meaning when it becomes a witness, when it evokes an admiration and conversion, and when it becomes the preaching and proclamation of the Good News. *(On Evangelization in the Modern World,* 15)

This period of evangelization or precatechumenate frequently begins before an inquirer formally approaches the church. Family, friends, neighbors and co-workers often are the catalyst that inspires an individual to ponder the depths of the spiritual life. Sometimes old assumptions are challenged by the good example and living faith of others. Sometimes a faith that has been dormant is stirred up by the witness of others. Catechumenate ministers need to be aware of this natural and informal process of evangelization.

The community's involvement in the precatechumenate is important for the effectiveness of all that the catechumenate ministers will do. The community is the living context within which the catechumenate team will proclaim the good news of the gospel. If the catechumenate ministers proclaim the gospel but have no examples to point to of how it is being lived, then it will be very difficult to proclaim a credible message.

Is Evangelization Needed Today?

We live in a society where the basic story of Christianity is fairly well known. Many of the inquirers already are baptized, and many are familiar with biblical stories and images. They may believe in God, pray and even come to worship with their Catholic spouses.

We cannot presume, however, that because someone believes in God, he or she has grasped the gospel message to the point where his or her life has been transformed.

The period of evangelization is a time for sharing the gospel in its simplicity while also communicating the profound message it holds. This is the time for inquirers to sort out their beliefs and assumptions about God, others, self, church and world. The scriptures, the revelation of God to people of every age, will be the most important tool during this period.

For the period of evangelization to be effective, those working with inquirers must take the time to listen carefully to them. Each person comes with a story that has been building throughout his or her life. Eventually the candidates will be helped to join their experiences to the word of God in such a way that they will see their own lives reflected in the scriptures. They gradually will begin to identify the movement of God in their own lives.

Listening

In our enthusiasm about sharing our faith, we may fail to listen well to the inquirers. This listening is crucial to building that trust which is the foundation for the entire initiation process.

The listening begins with a personal interview with each inquirer. In these initial interviews we learn their background, their values, their motives for pursuing this process, their beliefs, their fears and their expectations. We may discover that there has been a crisis that led the person to inquire about the church. We may even discern that what the church has to offer is not really what the individual is looking for.

Our listening requires respect for each individual. The unique history of each inquirer, including his or her religious convictions or perceptions, must be respected. It is the starting point in our ministry to them.

The quality of our listening will be just as important as the words we speak. Through our listening we extend a genuine welcome, an act of love that establishes an atmosphere of mutual respect and understanding. This interview is not a time for judgments and certainly not the time to begin a systematic theological review. It is a time for being aware of how God's grace is at work and to acknowledge that it is the Lord who takes the lead in this whole process.

While the art of listening is crucial for this first period, it is equally important for the entire process. Good listening can keep us from blindly going our own way and leaving candidates and catechumens behind.

Initial Conversion

The goal of the precatechumenate period is initial conversion, the beginning of a turn from old ways and beliefs to the living Christ, to the reign of God and to the church.

Conversion to the Living Christ Christian conversion is a meeting of the person with the living Christ. The ministers of initiation introduce the inquirer to the person of Christ through honest dialogue, exposure to the scriptures, personal sharing and witnessing. But the inquirer must reach out to Christ when he or she is ready. This may take a long time, or it may already be evident in the inquirer's life. The inquirers must be supported lovingly and patiently until they are ready.

Conversion to the Reign of God While many inquirers are believers in Christ, there is still the call to conversion to the reign of God that Jesus preached. Christian conversion sometimes can be incomplete; one can hold firmly to a personal, intimate relationship with Christ but pay little attention to Christ's word.

Jesus did not establish an elite following for himself. He preached the reign of God, which is "a kingdom of holiness and grace, a kingdom of justice, love and peace" (Preface, Christ the King). This kingdom is a radical challenge to contemporary society, and thus to the inquirer.

In the kingdom Jesus preached, the first shall be last and the greatest will be the servant of all. We are not to worry about what we are to wear or eat. We must love our enemies and pray for our persecutors. The poor and the peacemakers are the blessed ones in the kingdom. Such a kingdom is a far cry from the materialism, sexism, consumerism and violence of the society we call home today. But the kingdom is not just a dream for the hereafter. Jesus said the reign of God is in our midst, has broken into our history.

Our evangelizing in this first period of the initiation process is not only to introduce Jesus but also to proclaim the kingdom he stands for and to face the conversion it demands of us. Jim Wallis has commented on the close relationship between conversion and the reign of God:

> Conversion in the New Testament can only be understood from the perspective of the kingdom of God. The salvation of individuals and the fulfillment of the kingdom are intimately connected and are linked in the preaching of Jesus and the apostles. The powerful and compelling call to conversion in the gospels arose directly out of the fact of an inbreaking new order. To be converted to Christ meant to give one's allegiance to the kingdom, to enter into God's purposes for the world expressed in the language of the kingdom. The disciples couldn't have given themselves to Jesus and then ignored the meaning of his kingdom for their lives and the world. Their conversion, like ours, can only be understood from the vantage point of the new age inaugurated in Jesus Christ. They joined him, followed him, transferred their allegiance to him, and, in so doing, became people of the new order. His gospel was the good news of the kingdom of God. There is no other gospel in the New Testament. The arrival of Jesus was the arrival of the kingdom.

> Our conversion, then, cannot be an end in itself; it is the first step of entry into the kingdom. Conversion marks the birth of the movement out of a merely private existence into a public consciousness. Conversion is the beginning of active solidarity with the purpose of the kingdom of God in the world. No longer preoccupied with our private lives, we are engaged in a vocation for the world. Our prayer becomes, "Thy kingdom come, thy will be done, on earth as it is in heaven." If we restrict our salvation to only inner concerns, we have yet to enter into its fullness. Turning from ourselves to Jesus identifies us with him in the world. Conversion, then, is to public responsibility — but public responsibility as defined by the kingdom, not by the state. Our own salvation, which began with a personal decision about Jesus Christ, becomes intimately linked with the fulfillment of the kingdom of God. The connection between conversion and the kingdom cannot be emphasized enough. *(The Call to Conversion* [San Francisco: Harper & Row, 1981], 8–9)

Preaching the reign of God is not easy. We can expect the gospel message to disturb our minds and hearts as we wrestle with the vision of the kingdom. Neither the parish nor the catechumenate team can pretend to have mastered the challenges of conversion. We must humbly share the struggle to live for the kingdom. At first hearing, the reign of God may sound burdensome, but we know it can be liberating, life-giving and joyful. Those who work with inquirers must know these benefits of the kingdom through their own experience.

The kingdom we announce as truth and life will be hard to grasp if there is no evidence of it in the parish community. A parish must ask itself, "Are we any different from the rest of society? What do we stand for? Is it obvious?" Evangelization is not a scheduled period of time or an optional program but an ongoing characteristic of the community itself.

The church is an evangelizer. But it begins by being evangelized itself. The church is the community of believers, the community of hope lived and communicated, the community of brotherly love; and it needs to listen unceasingly to what it must believe, to its reasons for hoping, to the new commandment of love. The church is the people of God immersed in the world and often tempted by idols, and it always needs to hear the proclamation of the "mighty works of God" which converted it to the Lord. The church always needs to be called together afresh by him and to be reunited. *(On Evangelization in the Modern World, 15)*

Conversion to the Church   To be a Christian means that we join with other believers in building God's kingdom. We need one another to discover that the Lord is present to us as we work to build the kingdom.

The church is more than a religious institution. It is — we are — a sacrament, that is, an instrument through which we encounter the risen Lord. This underlies our Catholic tradition of liturgy and sacraments. The church is not a gathering of like-minded people but a diverse community gathered into one body with Christ as head.

During the period of evangelization, inquirers are drawn to a deeper experience of the church. They begin to see and reverence Christ living among us. As inquirers deepen their appreciation for the communal dimension of faith, they gradually begin to talk about the church as "we" rather than "you."

The conversion to the living Christ, to the reign of God and to the church, which we hope will occur during this first period, is only an initial conversion. During the catechumenate it will be deepened through catechesis, prayer and dialogue. In this first phase we will look for some signs of change taking place in the lives of the inquirers. That initial change will need careful direction and nurturing throughout the initiation process.

Other Issues during the Precatechumenate

While listening well and sharing the gospel message are at the heart of this period, we also can expect to find some interest on the part of the inquirers for "Catholic things." Inquirers often want to know right at the beginning what makes Catholics different from Presbyterians or Baptists or Jews. They may be eager to know why Catholics genuflect, celebrate reconciliation or light candles. They may be very curious about Catholic teaching on birth control, abortion or social justice.

There is a temptation to put off all these questions that seem either of little importance or too involved to explain in one session. While many questions or issues can be covered in more depth at a later time, there is good reason to address the issues at least briefly when they come up: It will help to build trust. It may also alleviate some blocks or hesitations or unreasonable fear of the church, which could keep someone from receiving the gospel message.

Just as we take time to listen to the personal life stories of each individual inquirer, it also is appropriate to share the story of the local parish during this period. What is its history? What is its mission? Who are its leaders?

In short, the period of evangelization may well be the least defined and the least ordered part of the initiation process. But so it must be. During this time, inquirers are looking the church over and trying to feel comfortable about being with us, catechumenate team members are trying to understand the inquirers better and to respond to their needs, and parishioners may be wondering what they can do for the inquirers. It is a period of negotiation and discovery. Hospitality, sincerity and credible witness, valuable throughout the process, are the basic tools for the precatechumenate.

The Length of the Precatechumenate

The length of the precatechumenate will depend on the background and needs of the inquirers. Some individuals may need very little before they are ready to move on to the period of the catechumenate. A time frame cannot be set arbitrarily. For example, it would be inappropriate to expect someone who is a deeply converted Christian to undergo a lengthy precatechumenate just because there are others who need a lengthy precatechumenate or because a plan is in place for a set number of sessions regardless of who the inquirers might be.

Conversely, there may be some individuals who need many months in an evangelization period. There may be a number of personal issues an inquirer needs to sort out before proceeding further. The process of conversion may be a genuine struggle and may proceed very slowly. The ideal solution to the time issue is to provide a precatechumenate that is ongoing. Perhaps a few parishioners could make the precatechumenate their special ministry, opening their living room one night a week all year long for the precatechumenate. In this way, no matter when an inquirer arrives and no matter when he or she is ready to move on to the catechumenate, there will be a forum that addresses his or her needs.

Catechumenate

After giving some evidence of an initial conversion and a genuine desire to pursue initiation into the Catholic church, inquirers are invited to participate in the catechumenate period.

Determining the readiness for this period is an important responsibility of the catechumenate ministry. Through a series of personal interviews and through careful listening in group sessions, someone from the catechumenate team helps each inquirer discern his or her motives and readiness to move along the process of initiation.

The *Rite of Christian Initiation of Adults* offers a basic outline upon which the discernment rests:

> Thus there must be evidence of the first faith that was conceived during the period of evangelization and precatechumenate and of an initial conversion and intention to change their lives and to enter into a relationship with God in Christ. Consequently, there must also be evidence of the first stirring of repentance, a start to the practice of calling upon God in prayer, a sense of the church, and some experience of the company and spirit of Christians through contact with a priest or with members of the community. (42)

Becoming a Catechumen

The Rite of Acceptance into the Order of Catechumens marks the passage from the precatechumenate into the catechumenate period. During this rite, celebrated in the midst of the assembly, inquirers make a public promise to follow the way of Jesus, and they commit themselves to the formation process that leads to the initiation sacraments. The church in turn promises to support the inquirers, now called catechumens, and to help them know and follow Christ.

At the doors of the church the catechumens are marked with the sign of the cross. With this ancient sign they are claimed for Christ. They must learn to carry the cross throughout their lives. The community must help them to understand the cross not as a sign of defeat but as the Christian's sign of hope and life.

The catechumens are then invited into the assembly to hear the proclamation of the scriptures. The word of God is the foundation on which the catechumenate is built. During this rite the catechumens may receive a copy of the scriptures as a reminder that they are to build their lives upon the living word of God.

After the assembly prays for the new catechumens, they are led to another place where they continue their reflection upon the word of God. Because they are not yet able to share at the eucharistic table, their dismissal from the assembly is an invitation to be fed by the presence of the Lord in the sacred scriptures. Ordinarily the catechumens will be dismissed in this fashion each time the full assembly gathers for Mass.

The Rite of Acceptance into the Order of Catechumens can be celebrated any time that there are inquirers to take this step. The rite may be celebrated more than once in the year.

Once the inquirers have been accepted into the order of catechumens through this rite, they are considered part of the household of Christ (47). Their initial conversion and their desire to pursue a thorough formation in preparation for the sacraments of initiation already gives them a place within the church. Embraced by the church, they are supported by prayers, blessings and other rites. They are entitled to celebrate their marriages in the church; should someone die as a catechumen, he or she receives a Christian burial.

For those inquirers who are baptized, there is a rite parallel to the Rite of Acceptance that marks their passage into the catechumenate period. The Rite of Welcoming Candidates (411–433) recognizes that these individuals have already been baptized. "Now the church surrounds them with special care and support as they prepare to be sealed with the gift of the Spirit in confirmation and take their place at the banquet table of Christ's sacrifice." (412)

The candidates' participation in the rite is an acknowledgment on their part that God has been at work in their lives and that they are eager to deepen their commitment to Christ and his gospel. The prayers in the Rite of Welcoming Candidates capture the spirit of what lies ahead for the candidates: "That these candidates may come to a deeper appreciation of the gift of their baptism, which joined them to Christ. . . ." (430)

Elements of the Catechumenate Period

The *Rite of Christian Initiation of Adults* outlines four primary means by which the church fosters the conversion and Christian formation of catechumens and candidates (75):

- a suitable catechesis accommodated to the liturgical year
- becoming familiar with the Christian way of life by the example and support of the community
- the celebration of liturgical rites
- apprenticeship in the apostolic life and mission of the church.

A Suitable Catechesis Accommodated to the Liturgical Year

The order of initiation describes a catechesis that is thorough and helps the catechumens and candidates reach a profound sense of the mystery of salvation. This catechesis is offered by priests, deacons, catechists and others in the community, who by sharing the living faith of the church help to enlighten the faith of catechumens and candidates.

The purpose of the catechesis is not to form theologians or church historians but to form men and women in the wisdom and tradition of the church in a way that gives reason to faith and enables them to live by faith in the midst of the world.

Catechesis helps catechumens and candidates find meaning in their own experiences of life. By our sharing of the richness of our biblical and doctrinal heritage, they are gradually helped to value the Catholic tradition which they will claim as their own.

Catechesis during this period is not merely doctrinal instruction. While the doctrine of the church must be communicated, it is essential that catechumens learn what the church's teachings mean for their lives individually and as part of the church community. This understanding of catechesis suitable for catechumens does not result in a loosely structured sharing group where there are no goals or expectations. A catechumenal community is not a sensitivity group that makes feelings or emotions the primary concern. The dialogue and process that are part of the catechumenate surely will respect people's feelings and invite them to share the story of their lives, but it does not end there. As the *Rite of Christian Initiation of Adults* states, "This catechesis leads the catechumens not only to an appropriate acquaintance with dogmas and precepts but also to a profound sense of the mystery of salvation in which they desire to participate." (75)

The methods of catechesis used during this time must respect the way adults learn. Catechists and other initiation ministers must keep the purpose of the catechumenate in mind and remember that growth and development in the Christian life is a lifelong process.

Lectionary-based Catechesis Because catechesis during the catechumenate is based both on the church's teachings and traditions and on the catechumens' experiences, no book, class syllabus or lesson plan can be created to suit the needs of every catechumenate group or every catechumen.

The most effective means of catechesis during this period is lectionary-based catechesis, in which the Sunday scriptures are the ground upon which a solid, doctrinal catechesis is built. In practice this means that after the catechumens and candidates have had the opportunity to hear and reflect upon the word of

God, a catechist will lead them to discover the basic Catholic teachings contained, implied or suggested in the scriptures. This enables the catechumens and candidates to see how church teaching is rooted in the scripture.

This method also introduces the catechumens and candidates into the rhythm and grace of the liturgical year. The feasts and seasons of the church year unfold the profound mystery of Christ day by day. Learning to use the scriptures in this way provides the catechumens and candidates with a method of ongoing spiritual growth and enlightenment from which they can draw for the rest of their lives.

People who are not acquainted with lectionary-based catechesis are sometimes skeptical about whether this type of catechesis is sufficient to cover the wealth of Catholic teaching. It is. But it may not follow a systematic or historical approach to doctrinal formation.

Lectionary-based catechesis is recommended as the primary method of catechesis, but not the only method. Some diversity in approach may be helpful and welcomed by the candidates and catechumens. If a catechumenate team that employs lectionary-based catechesis begins to feel anxious about something that is not being addressed, there is no reason not to deal with that issue.

The *General Catechetical Directory*, the *National Catechetical Directory* and the *Catechism of the Catholic Church* are valuable tools for the catechist. From these documents the catechist will be able to grasp the scope of what needs to be taught, and how.

The Length of the Catechumenate   Because the length of the catechumenate depends on the needs of the catechumens, there is no predetermined amount of time prescribed. The natural inclination in North America is to follow a school-year calendar and force the catechumenate period into a short time frame, from late autumn to the beginning of Lent. This is usually not enough time to provide a thorough and solid catechetical formation. The statutes regarding the catechumenate in the United States direct that the catechumenate period "should extend at least one year of formation, instruction and probation. Ordinarily this period should go from at least the Easter Season of one year until the next; preferably it should begin before Lent in one year and extend until Easter of the following year" (U.S. Statutes, 7).

Baptized candidates preparing for reception into full communion may or may not need as extensive a catechumenate period as catechumens. The length of the period for candidates depends entirely on their background, level of understanding and personal integration of the church's teaching.

Parishes are gradually finding that an ongoing catechumenate is most effective. Using the lectionary as the catechetical base easily facilitates an ongoing catechumenate. In this way, individual catechumens and candidates can enter and leave this period depending on their own situation.

Becoming Familiar with the Christian Way of Life   Catechumens and candidates need the support and living witness of the community in addition to catechetical formation. By meeting and getting to know mature Catholics, catechumens and candidates will learn how Catholic tradition, values and customs are lived day by day. By interacting with members of the community, catechumens and candidates will be exposed to various expressions of Catholic spirituality, styles of personal prayer, family customs and ethnic traditions. There is a great deal of diversity within the unity of the church. Catechumens and candidates should be given the opportunity to appreciate the full Catholic experience.

A welcoming community provides an environment that allows catechumens and candidates to explore the richness of the Christian tradition as they gradually apply it to themselves and accept it as their own. Welcoming the new Catholic by offering hospitality, support and interest is the human expression of the truth that we initiate people not into a theological abstraction but into the body of Christ, the community of faith. The community's interaction and involvement with catechumens and candidates makes this principle come alive.

The faith and witness of a friend, co-worker or member of the family most often is what first led the catechumen or candidate to investigate the Christian life. The community builds on that experience. For those who come from a background that is unsupportive or even hostile to Christian life, the care of the community will be crucial.

There is, of course, no program for how a community will interact with catechumens and candidates. While catechumenal teams may provide opportunities for catechumens and candidates to meet other Catholics, such interaction usually will take place outside the formal sessions; parish social events are great opportunities for catechumens and candidates to meet other Catholics. Sponsors especially can introduce catechumens and candidates to various members of the community. The sponsor or a team member might ask someone to accompany a catechumen to a meeting or prayer service that the catechumen (or parish member) might be hesitant to attend alone.

The Celebration of Liturgical Rites   Another component of the catechumenate period is participation in the church's liturgical life. Liturgy is not simply one thing among many that a community does; liturgy is the source and the summit of Christian life. In the liturgy we encounter the living Christ, the revelation of God, the source of our strength for living the Christian life. We bring to the liturgy all that we are and all that we have tried to do in the Lord's name. At this summit where we join our daily sacrifices to Christ's, we and our world are transformed.

The liturgy is also the church's creed. We pray what we believe. Over the course of a lifetime the liturgy shapes our minds and hearts individually and collectively.

Because the liturgy is so essential to the church's identity, it is important to introduce new Catholics to the liturgical life of the church thoroughly and gradually. By participating in various rites and liturgical experiences, the catechumens and candidates will gain an appreciation for the church's liturgy, but, more importantly, they will be formed by what they pray.

The liturgy of the word is the primary liturgy for catechumens and candidates. In the liturgy of the word they will experience the presence of Christ in the proclamation of his word. Week by week and year by year the catechumens and candidates — and all Christians — are called to make the scriptures the foundation of their Christian lives. A liturgy of the word may also be a suitable context for catechesis to take place. The *Rite of Christian Initiation of Adults* (81 – 89) provides an outline for celebrations of the word of God apart from the celebration of the eucharist.

The liturgical rites outlined in the *Rite of Christian Initiation of Adults* are not optional or arbitrarily chosen to give some variety to the months of the catechumenate. These rites mark transitions between stages and growth in the Christian life. Good ritual communicates the mystery of Christ in ways that words alone cannot. Among these rites are blessings (95 – 97), minor exorcisms (90–94), anointing with the oil of catechumens (98–103), and presentations of the Creed and Lord's Prayer (104–105). All of these rites surround the catechumens and candidates with the prayer, love and support of the church.

The liturgical rites should be integrated into the catechetical formation so that prayer, ritual and scripture flow from and are compatible with catechesis, which will in turn build upon the rites that have been celebrated.

Many catechumenate teams place great emphasis on spontaneous shared prayer during the time of formation. This is a laudable practice, but care must be taken not to neglect liturgical prayer. The liturgy of the church is the basic source of spiritual life. After the sacraments of initiation have been celebrated, catechumens and candidates may not have a small community like the catechumenate to pray and share with, but they always will have the church's liturgy to guide them.

The task, then, is to show catechumens and candidates how to make the liturgy their own prayer. If we do this, we will have given the gift that enables constant growth in faith. Catechumens and candidates ought to be introduced gradually to the many facets of Catholic prayer and ritual, including the feasts and seasons (liturgical year), and the liturgy of the hours. They should be assisted in learning how to make liturgical words, songs and gestures true prayers of the heart.

Catechumens and candidates are encouraged to carry the spirit of liturgical prayer, and the feasts and the seasons of the church and life, into the home.

Apprenticeship in the Apostolic Life and Mission of the Church

The formation of catechumens and candidates should lead them to work actively with others to spread the gospel and build the kingdom of God. This expectation flows from the church's understanding that baptism and confirmation closely join us to the ministry of Jesus and that eucharist compels us to break the bread of our lives for others in memory of Christ.

In the past, the church may not have given this aspect of initiation sufficient attention. Baptism most often was understood almost exclusively as something done for an individual's personal salvation. Baptism as commitment to service in Jesus' name often was overlooked. By introducing the catechumens and candidates into the apostolic life of the church, our practice of initiation strikes a better balance between the personal and the communal.

Christian initiation is a personal participation in the saving act of Christ. But baptism, confirmation and eucharist are not only for one's own spiritual benefit. Through our participation in the sacraments of initiation we are conformed to Christ as his disciples and sent into the world to further the reign of God.

Catechumens learn best what it means to serve from those already engaged in service, but finding groups for catechumens to serve with may be difficult in some parishes. If so, the parish may need to review its commitment to service in Jesus' name.

Such service should not be limited to various ministries exercised in the sanctuary or parish center. The world is the Christian's sanctuary, and it is in the world that we are called to build God's kingdom. Catechumenate teams need to witness and join others in Christian service beyond the parish. Men and women involved in visiting the sick and the imprisoned, or in caring for the elderly and the poor — and others, too, who understand their mission as Christians in quite ordinary ways — are the people catechumens and candidates need to meet and learn from. The Christian vocation must be exercised beyond the parish center: in businesses and neighborhoods, schools and social and political arenas. The resources of the diocese, a Catholic Worker House, the Bread for the World movement, Pax Christi and other such groups could be drawn on for suggestions; these groups may even welcome catechumens and candidates to join them in their work. Pope John Paul II's exhortation to the laity, *Christifideles Laici*, is valuable in understanding the role of the baptized Christian in the world.

> The images of salt, light and leaven taken from the gospel, although indiscriminately applicable to all Jesus' disciples, are specifically applied to the lay faithful. They are particularly meaningful images, because they speak not only of the deep involvement and the full participation of the lay faithful in the affairs of the earth, the world and the human community, but also and above all, they tell of an involvement and participation which has its purpose the spreading of the gospel that brings salvation. (*Christifidelis Laici*, 15)

Purification and Enlightenment

The third phase of the initiation process is the period of purification and enlightenment. This coincides with Lent, a season of penance and conversion leading to baptism or baptismal renewal at Easter. During this time, the catechumens reflect on their faith and religious experience in an intense manner. They take all that they have heard and seen, learned, prayed and shared, and they ponder it all in the depths of their hearts. Lent supports this process of interiorizing, giving it shape and direction through the scriptures, prayers and traditional lenten disciplines of fasting, doing works of charity and penance, and offering personal sacrifice.

Rite of Election

The period of purification and enlightenment begins with the Rite of Election on or near the First Sunday of Lent. Here the church states its intention to baptize the catechumens at Easter. The rite presumes that the church is certain of several things: that the catechumens' conversion has matured, that their minds and morals are Christlike, that the practice of faith and charity is evident in their daily lives. These catechumens are not expected to be perfect, but it must be evident that the way of Jesus is becoming their way of life even though they must still deal with their own faults, hesitations and sinfulness.

> Before the Rite of Election is celebrated, the catechumens are expected to have undergone a conversion in mind and in action and to have developed a sufficient acquaintance with Christian teaching as well as a spirit of faith and charity. With deliberate will and an enlightened faith they must have the intention to receive the sacraments of the church, a resolve they will express publicly in the actual celebration of the rite. (120)

The questions asked of godparents during the rite give some indication of what is expected before the catechumens are chosen for the initiation sacraments. The bishop inquires

> Have they faithfully listened to the word of God proclaimed by the church? Have they been true to the word they have received and begun to walk in God's presence? Have they sought the fellowship of their brothers and sisters and joined them in prayer? (131)

These questions summarize the dialogue that is to take place between catechumens and their catechumenal communities long before the celebration of the rite. Before the invitation to celebrate the Rite of Election is extended, the catechumen meets with one or more members of the catechumenate team to discuss the catechumen's readiness. The task of the church at this time — carried out by the bishop, pastor, catechist and sponsors — is to discern in the catechumens a genuine response to the call to Christian discipleship.

Catechumenal ministers must take this discernment process seriously. While the idea of choosing people for initiation may seem to some, especially those who place a high value on privacy and individualism, to be elitist, the church would be remiss in initiating an individual for whom the catechumenal process has made no difference or who is not yet ready to participate fully in the church's life. When it seems that an individual's disposition or motives for initiation are not clear to us or to the individual, we have a responsibility to question that person's readiness.

This discernment is not a judgment made hastily or by surprise. There ought to be discussions throughout the process, which naturally come to a point of decision prior to the celebration of the Rite of Election.

Just as we can take the discernment process too lightly, so can we become too idealistic or unreasonable in our expectations of catechumens. We are not making a judgment on their sanctity but on their readiness for the Christian life. Catechumenal ministers will find the discernment process challenging to their own faith. Their awareness of their own need for growth should help them be more realistic in their expectations of the catechumens.

The bishop usually presides over the Rite of Election. As pastor of the diocesan church, the bishop formally chooses, or "elects," men and women for the celebration of the sacraments of initiation at the Easter Vigil. This election is reminiscent of Israel's election by God to be a people of the covenant. The Rite of Election carries with it the echo of Jesus' words, "I have

chosen you, you have not chosen me." As the names of the catechumens are called and enrolled in the Book of the Elect, catechumens and assembly are reminded that these catechumens are known by God and personally called by name.

When the bishop presides over a diocesan celebration of the rite of election at the cathedral church or in the regions of the diocese, it becomes clear that the catechumens are being chosen for initiation into a church that extends beyond the parish communities from which they come. They are being called to membership in the universal church, for which they must also show their concern.

In preparation for the Rite of Election a parish may wish to celebrate a Rite of Sending the Catechumens for Election (106–117). This rite allows the local community to hear the testimony of sponsors and catechists on behalf of the catechumens and to support them with their prayers. The catechumens are sent to the Rite of Election knowing the support and affirmation of their own community.

Call to Continuing Conversion
The edition of the *Rite of Christian Initiation of Adults* approved for use in the United States provides a celebration for baptized candidates that is parallel to the Rite of Election. Because they are already baptized, candidates who are completing their initiation through the sacraments of confirmation and eucharist, and candidates for reception into full communion are already God's elect. Nevertheless, their desire to deepen their faith and strengthen their membership in the church can be celebrated in the Call to Continuing Conversion (450–458). This rite may be celebrated in the parish or it may be combined with the diocesan celebration of the Rite of Election (550–561).

The questions that the celebrant asks the sponsors in this rite indicate what ministry to the candidates prior to the celebration of this rite involves and the criteria we use to discern their readiness for the sacraments:

> Have they faithfully listened to the apostles' instruction proclaimed by the church? Have they come to a deeper appreciation of their baptism, in which they were joined to Christ and his church? Have they reflected sufficiently on the tradition of the church, which is their heritage, and joined their brothers and sisters in prayer? (453)

When combined rites — those that include both catechumens and candidates — are celebrated, every effort must be made to avoid any confusion that would blur the distinction between the baptized and the unbaptized. Failing to make that distinction weakens the appreciation of the dignity of Christian baptism and is ecumenically offensive.

Examination of Life

From Ash Wednesday to Holy Thursday, the entire church community reexamines its life. Lent is a time to cleanse ourselves of what may still stand in the way of living for the kingdom of God. Lent enlightens and uncovers the truth — the true way of life, the true path to holiness, the radical kingdom of God to which we are called.

Several traditional elements help us achieve these lenten ideals. Fasting and abstaining involve the whole person. Works of charity and almsgiving remedy the self-centered mind-set that can so easily entrap us. Penitential acts and prayers are humble admissions that we have sinned.

Lent is not so much a time for catechesis as it is a retreat preparing us for the initiation sacraments of Easter. This period finds its direction in the liturgy. The lectionary and sacramentary are the guides for the lenten journey.

Just as the parish's lenten discipline will affect the lives of the elect (the title now given to the catechumens who will be initiated at the coming Easter) and candidates, they in turn can have a powerful impact on the assembly. The elect and candidates are themselves the primary symbol for Lent. We see in them what we ought to see happening in ourselves: a conversion that leaves us with a hunger for eucharist and a thirst for building the kingdom.

This conversion is strengthened and deepened in the scrutinies and exorcisms, which take place on the Third, Fourth and Fifth Sundays of Lent. "Scrutiny" may seem an odd word to use in this situation, but it describes well what happens when the word of God is proclaimed. That word searches our hearts and scrutinizes our values and way of life. This scrutinizing happens outside the formal rites — throughout Lent and long before — as the elect search their lives in the light of the gospel and so identify the falsehood that keeps them from the kingdom of God.

When the evils, temptations and falsehoods from which we need to be freed have been identified through such scrutiny, there is need for exorcism. These evils are forceful obstacles to our living for the kingdom of God. They include some of the most powerful forces of our age: materialism, consumerism, sexism, racism, militarism, hedonism and idolatry in many forms. These are the cultural demons that hold men and women in bondage and so frustrate the building of God's kingdom.

The exorcism prayers in the *Rite of Christian Initiation of Adults* are somewhat generic. They speak of falsehood, blindness, evil, the father of lies. For these words to have meaning, the elect must be helped to name the falsehood and blindness of their lives. These words also tell what ought to be happening in Lent for all the members of the church: renunciation of the demons. Exorcisms are not primarily rites of forgiveness or reconciliation but of liberation. During the celebration of the scrutiny, the elect and the baptized members of the community may recognize that they have given in to evils that have blinded them. For this the exorcism prayers ask forgiveness, but it is baptism for the unbaptized, and penance and eucharist for the already baptized, that will serve as sacramental cleansing of sin.

The exorcism prayers of the Rite of Scrutiny were composed for catechumens, thus the imagery in the prayers refers to the preparation for baptism. The text of initiation favors reserving the scrutinies and exorcisms on the Third, Fourth and Fifth Sundays of Lent for the unbaptized (463).

The U.S. edition of the *Rite of Christian Initiation of Adults* includes a penitential rite that is designed in the spirit of a scrutiny (459 – 472) for baptized candidates. This rite may be celebrated on the Second Sunday of Lent or on a lenten weekday. This penitential rite helps to prepare the candidates for the celebration of the sacrament of penance. The statutes regulating the practice of Christian initiation in the United States encourage the celebration of the sacrament of penance prior to and distinct from the celebration of the rite of reception into the full communion of the Catholic church (U.S. Statutes, 36).

Preparatory Rites on Holy Saturday

Those who are to be initiated at the Easter Vigil are encouraged to gather for prayer during the day of Holy Saturday. Catechumens and candidates, along with the entire community, are instructed to keep and extend the paschal fast of Good Friday throughout Holy Saturday until the end of the Vigil itself (U.S. Statutes, 15 and canon 1251). This is not a penitential fast but a fast of joy and anticipation of the sacred mysteries.

Several rites are recommended for use on Holy Saturday during the day, although not all of these rites would necessarily be used. Local needs and culture may suggest which are the most appropriate to celebrate and how.

Rites that may be used include the Recitation of the Creed (193–196), Ephphetha Rite (197–199) and Choosing a Baptismal Name (200–205). An anointing with the oil of catechumens (98–103) may also be used for the unbaptized, if pastorally appropriate. A model for a celebration of the preparation rites is offered (187–192).

The Easter Vigil and the Sacraments of Christian Initiation

The focus of the Easter Vigil is on Jesus Christ dead and risen. It is not a testimonial to the candidates. The candidates for baptism and reception into the church show us, in their transformation this night, that Christ has indeed been raised. He has given us new life through his victory over sin and death. In his dying and rising we see more clearly the shape of our own lives.

The liturgy of baptism takes place after the homily. The candidates for baptism are called by name and come forward with their godparents. As the litany of saints is chanted, the deacon takes the paschal candle and leads the catechumens to the font.

After a solemn blessing of the baptismal water, the presider invites the candidates for baptism to renounce all evil and to profess their faith in the Father, the Son and the Holy Spirit. The whole process of the catechumenate reaches a climax as the candidates publicly profess the faith they intend to live for the rest of their lives.

Baptism follows immediately. Immersion is the preferred way of baptizing. "Christian Initiation, General Introduction" states, "Either the rite of immersion, which is more suitable as a symbol of participation in the death and resurrection of Christ, or the rite of infusion may lawfully be used in the celebration of baptism." (22) *Environment and Art in Catholic Worship*, from the Bishops' Committee on the Liturgy, echoes this view:

> To speak of symbols and of sacramental significance is to indicate that immersion is the fuller and more appropriate symbolic action in baptism. New baptismal fonts, therefore, should be constructed to allow for the immersion of infants, at least, and to allow for the pouring of water over the entire body of a child or adult. (76)

The newly baptized are clothed in a baptismal robe or gown. Godparents may assist in the vesting. When baptism is by total immersion, the newly baptized may be taken to adjacent rooms where they dress in their baptismal robes before returning to the assembly. They then are presented with a candle lit from the Easter candle.

Renewal of Baptismal Promises

The celebrant then invites the candidates for reception into full communion to join the community in a solemn renewal of baptismal promises. Holding lit candles in their hands, the candidates and community publicly renounce sin and reject Satan. Then they all profess their faith in the Trinity. These are the vows of baptism, the vows upon which our Christian discipleship rests and upon which our unity and identity as the body of Christ, the church, is built.

After a sprinkling with the baptismal water, the candidates for reception into full communion are invited to state their belief and commitment to the Roman Catholic church (585). Then the celebrant formally welcomes them into the full communion of the Catholic church (586; see also 473 – 504). The newly baptized, those received into full communion and those Catholics completing their Christian initiation are now confirmed (587 – 591). (The celebration of reception into full communion and of confirmation and eucharist for Catholics completing their Christian initiation also may take place at times other than the Easter Vigil.)

The order of Christian initiation and the code of canon law stress the importance of celebrating confirmation immediately after baptism so that, with the eucharist, these sacraments will be seen and understood as one integral action of Christ initiating new members into his church.

> In accord with the ancient practice followed in the Roman liturgy, adults are not to be baptized without receiving confirmation immediately afterward, unless some serious reason stands in the way. The conjunction of the two celebrations signifies the unity of the paschal mystery, the close link between the mission of the Son and the outpouring of the Holy Spirit, and the connection of the two sacraments through which the Son and the Holy Spirit come with the Father to those who are baptized. (215)

> In order to signify clearly the interrelation or coalescence of the three sacraments which are required for full Christian initiation (canon 842:2), adult candidates, including children of catechetical age, are to receive baptism, confirmation and eucharist in a single eucharistic celebration, whether at the Easter Vigil or, if necessary, at some other time. (U.S. Statutes, 14)

First Sharing in the Celebration of the Eucharist

After the newly initiated are sealed with the gift of the Holy Spirit, they are led to the eucharistic table. "With the entire community they share in the offering of the sacrifice and say the Lord's Prayer, giving expression to the spirit of adoption as God's children." (217) Now sharing in the royal priesthood of Christ, the neophytes (as the newly baptized are called) may participate in the general intercessions and be invited to bring the gifts of bread and wine to the altar.

Participation in the eucharist means that these new Catholics can claim the eucharistic prayer as their own. One with the priestly baptized community, they enter ever more deeply into the dying and rising of the Lord, whose flesh and blood seals their participation in the new covenant. The eucharist is the repeatable sacrament of initiation, which draws the baptized with every eucharist into the heart of the paschal mystery. Every celebration of the eucharist, then, is an opportunity to renew what was begun in baptism and confirmation.

Postbaptismal Catechesis

The final period in the initiation process is postbaptismal catechesis, or mystagogy (which means "teaching the mysteries," that is, the sacraments). We might be inclined to consider the initiation process completed with the Easter Vigil, but the order of initiation provides yet another moment in the whole process: a time for new members to adjust to their vocation within the church and to deepen their understanding of the paschal mystery by drawing from their experience of the community and the sacraments (244–251 and U.S. Statutes, 22–24).

This postbaptismal period can be difficult for the newly received members of the church. The rites of the catechumenate and the Vigil are past, primary catechesis is completed, and the community, which at one time was so involved with the candidates, seems to be less in evidence. There often is a letdown.

For the new members, the season of Easter is crucial. Not only do they need to know that the community is still interested in them but they need to find their place in its ordinary daily life. The new members, fresh in their experience of the Easter sacraments, are ripe for a deeper journey into the sacramental dimension of life.

The most appropriate place for mystagogical catechesis is at the Sunday Masses. The scriptures and prayers of the Easter Season are a gradual unfolding of the meaning and implications of the sacraments of baptism, confirmation and eucharist. The homilist can draw from the richness of the Easter symbols and sacramental celebrations that are still fresh in the memory of the congregation.

Many find this period of the initiation process the most difficult to implement in the parish. This may be due to an inability in our culture to reflect upon past experience. We eagerly anticipate what is to come, and we enthusiastically engage in what is at hand, but once the waited-for event is past, we tend to move on to other things. This lack of reflection affects many dimensions of life, including our commitment to Christ and his gospel.

Parish ministers must be patient in developing this post-baptismal period. In addition to the celebration of Sunday eucharist, opportunities for sharing and praying in less structured settings may be helpful. Some have found that sharing insights and memories of the catechumenate and Easter Vigil happen naturally at a festive meal or a party during the Easter Season.

In developing an effective mystagogy we need to look for mystagogues — individuals who have a special gift for uncovering what we know by experience or believe in the heart. Some of the early Fathers of the church were great mystagogues. Reading some of the homilies and letters of Cyril of Jerusalem, Ambrose of Milan, or Theodore of Mopsuestia will provide insight into the deeper levels of the meaning and experience of sacramental life. What is evident in the writings of these mystagogues is their poetry and their careful attention to symbol. This is not a time for the kind of theological analysis one might expect in a classroom. Rather, it is a time to encourage the deeply human and spiritual expressions of those who have had a profound experience that can only be explained by faith.

The period of mystagogy will be most effective in communities where the 50 days of Easter are celebrated well. The Easter Season itself becomes the environment in which mystagogy takes place. These 50 days ought to be filled with festivity and beauty, parties and special celebrations. The music, art and decoration, preaching and liturgy of Easter are all important for giving mystagogy its proper framework.

The Easter Season also is an appropriate time for the bishop to celebrate the eucharist with the newly initiated of the diocese (251). This is an occasion for the diocesan church to give thanks to God for the life that the newly initiated bring to the church. At such a celebration the bishop may congratulate and joyfully welcome the newly initiated into the eucharistic community. Like the Rite of Election, this is an opportunity for the bishop to establish a pastoral relationship with the newly initiated and to point to the universal dimension of church membership united under a common shepherd.

In the United States, the bishops' conference has determined that the period of mystagogy should extend for a full year, until the anniversary of initiation (U.S. Statutes, 24). The bishops have suggested that it may be helpful to assemble the newly initiated at least monthly for ongoing formation and pastoral care.

Because each new Catholic's needs will be different from another's, there is a caution about establishing too formal or rigid a structure for mystagogy. The key is pastoral care. Parish staff, catechumenate team, and especially godparents will perform an important ministry by keeping contact with the newly initiated. Through sensitive pastoral care we can discover what the newly initiated need, lead them into closer communion with church, foster a deeper exploration of the mysteries and support a wholesome and integrated Catholic Christian lifestyle.

Ministries:

The Call to Serve

Extended to All

The initiation of new members into the church involves the whole community. The *Rite of Christian Initiation of Adults* states emphatically:

> The people of God, as represented by the local church, should understand and show by their concern that the initiation of adults is the responsibility of all the baptized. Therefore the community must always be fully prepared in the pursuit of its apostolic vocation to give help to those who are searching for Christ. (9)

The baptized have the responsibility of spreading the faith according to their individual capabilities. The faithful play an important role by taking catechumens and candidates into their circles, openly discussing faith and Christian life, praying with them and for them, giving honest and prudent testimony about them and actively participating in the liturgical celebrations in the initiation process. A community's hospitality and its witness to gospel values will greatly help catechumens and candidates become active participants in the church's life and mission. If the catechumens and candidates feel welcomed only by a handful of ministers, their integration into the Christian community will be incomplete. They should sense the interest and charity of the whole congregation because it is into the whole community, not into the team of pastoral ministers, that catechumens and candidates are being initiated.

Many Catholics, however, do not see that they have any responsibility for initiating new members. Perhaps they live their faith very privately and do not feel any bond between themselves and other members of the community. Or perhaps they feel that they have never been welcomed into the community. These people may even resent that so much is being done for new Catholics when no one has extended any hospitality to them or offered them any of the opportunities for conversion and spiritual growth given so readily to inquirers, catechumens and candidates. The formation of communities that understand and appreciate the meaning of their own baptism and their bond with one another is an ongoing task, and one that is crucial to the success of a community-centered process of initiation. A parish that is conscious of its baptismal identity and that exercises its vocation in prayer, community life, gospel witness, charity and mission is the ideal setting for the catechumenate.

While the whole believing community takes responsibility for welcoming new Catholics, certain members of the community are asked to assume additional responsibilities for the care of the catechumens and candidates.

Sponsors

The *Rite of Christian Initiation of Adults* describes sponsors as "persons who have known and assisted the candidates and stand as witnesses to the candidates' moral character, faith and intention" (10). Later the text adds:

> Helped by the example and support of sponsors, godparents and the entire Christian community, the catechumens learn to turn more readily to God in prayer, to bear witness to the faith, in all things to keep their hope set on Christ, to follow the supernatural inspiration in their deeds, and to practice love of neighbor, even at the cost of self-renunciation. (75.2)

Through the sponsor, the catechumen or candidate will experience most directly the spirit and belief of the community. The sponsor ordinarily will be the one who introduces the catechumen or candidate to other members of the community and their various activities.

The *Rite of Christian Initiation of Adults* does not say whether a catechumen or candidate can have more than one sponsor, but there does not seem to be any reason why this could not be allowed. In some situations, for example, it might be desirable to have a family act as sponsor. The family would welcome the catechumen or candidate into their home, where the person could witness faith, hope and love in action. Most often, however, a catechumen or candidate will depend on one adult, someone he or she can trust and feel comfortable with.

Spouses ordinarily are not recommended as sponsors. While most candidates will naturally share important changes and insights with their spouses, there is a great value in the candidates' having someone outside the marriage with whom to share their spiritual journey. Spouses should, however, be invited to participate in the initiation process so that husbands and wives can grow together through the experience.

The sponsors should be approved by the pastoral team. They should be faithful Catholics who are comfortable relating with others are secure in their faith, and have a balanced spirituality and a love for the church. Sponsors ordinarily are chosen

from the parish by the catechumenate team, working in close collaboration with the pastoral staff.

The sponsor's responsibilities include: keeping in regular contact with the catechumens and candidates, encouraging them, listening to their questions and their doubts, sharing time and experience in a friendly manner, participating in the catechumenate sessions, praying with and for those they sponsor, and introducing them to the other members of the community. Sponsors may begin their ministry during the inquiry period, although they may not be assigned to a particular candidate until some months later.

A sponsor should assume sponsorship for one individual for as long as that might take. It is not advisable that the same people serve as sponsors year after year. Sponsorship belongs to the community, and the community is responsible for supplying sufficient sponsors each year. This will take time to develop as an expectation of the community.

The sponsor's role continues until the Rite of Election, when godparents begin to accompany the elect and the candidates to Easter sacraments. Sponsors do, however, continue to participate in the catechumenal community in support of the elect and the candidates. A sponsor also may be asked by the one he or she has sponsored to be his or her godparent.

Godparents

The ministry of the godparent is similar to that of the sponsor.

> Godparents are persons chosen by the candidates on the basis of example, good qualities and friendship, delegated by the local Christian community and approved by the priest. It is the responsibility of godparents to show the candidates how to practice the gospel in personal and social life, to

sustain the candidates in moments of hesitancy and anxiety, to bear witness and to guide the candidates' progress in the baptismal life. (11)

The godparent is similar to the sponsor in that he or she is expected to be a person of faith, to hold and live by Christian values, and to be capable of communicating faith and values to the elect or candidate.

Godparents assume their ministry at the Rite of Election and continue to fulfill that role for life. For this reason the godparent should be carefully selected. Godparents may be male or female, but they must be mature enough to undertake this responsibility; they must have received the three sacraments of initiation: baptism, confirmation and the eucharist; and they must be members of the Roman Catholic church free from any impediments or restrictions of church law that would keep them from carrying out their role.

Because the godparent offers testimony on behalf of the catechumen at the Rite of Election, it is presumed that the godparent already has a relationship to the catechumen. If the sponsor becomes the godparent, knowledge of the catechumen can be assured. In many cases a catechumen chooses a friend or family member as godparent. This existing relationship will have to be expanded to include the serious obligations of a godparent to a godchild. This must be discussed in the catechumenate community before the catechumens select godparents.

Candidates require a godparent for the sacrament of confirmation. In this case, the godparent's role may begin at the beginning of Lent with the ritual call to continuing conversion. In the event of a Catholic completing his or her Christian initiation, the godparent for confirmation may be the godparent from baptism.

The distinctions between sponsors and godparents continue to evolve. Different ethnic and cultural traditions also will have some bearing on these roles. What is important is that the roles of sponsors and godparents are understood as significant influences in the formation of catechumens and candidates.

Catechumenate Directors

Although it is the pastor's responsibility to oversee the order of Christian initiation and to see that the rites are celebrated with dignity and meaning, in many situations it is not practical for him to direct the day-to-day progress of the catechumenate. He should see to it that someone is appointed for this role who can facilitate the formation process, foster good communication and organize the efforts of all in the parish.

Catechumenate directors may be paid members of the parish staff or qualified volunteers. In either case, the director should receive the support and training necessary to exercise his or her role; diocesan pastoral services often are able to provide some assistance and direction. In many regions catechumenate directors meet regularly for professional growth and support.

Catechists

Catechists nurture the gift of faith. Respecting the presence of God to each individual, the catechist builds bridges between the experiences of life, the word of God, and the teaching and prayer of the church.

The catechist sets the direction and focus for individual catechetical sessions and for the catechetical process as a whole. The catechist must know the traditions and teachings of the church and appropriate methods for handing them on to adults. In addition, the catechist must be able to respond to the needs and mentality of a diverse group of catechumens and candidates, who may raise questions and issues in no particular order.

For those preparing for initiation, a lectionary-based style of catechesis best integrates catechesis with the liturgical year. The *National Catechetical Directory*, the *General Catechetical Directory* and the *Catechism of the Catholic Church* are important tools for catechists to use to ensure that connections are made from the word of God to the official teachings of the church. Catechists may wish to keep a record of all that has been taught and discussed so that a full scope of Catholic teaching is presented over the course of time.

> Catechists should see that their instruction is filled with the spirit of the gospel, adapted to the liturgical signs and the cycle of the church's year, suited to the needs of the catechumens, and as far as possible enriched by local traditions. (16)

Catechists represent the church to those they catechize. Therefore they must impart the church's beliefs and not simply their own opinions. Catechists should be well trained for their duties and be people of transparent faith. While catechists must be concerned about providing a thorough catechesis, they also must keep in mind that the presentation of teachings and precepts alone is not sufficient:

> The catechumenate means not simply a presentation of teachings and precepts, but a formation in the whole Christian life and a sufficiently prolonged period of training. *(Decree on the Church's Missionary Activity,* 14)

It is the bishop's responsibility to see that worthy catechists are prepared for this ministry. Vatican ii's *Decree on the Pastoral Office of Bishops in the Church* states that bishops

> should, furthermore, ensure that catechists are adequately prepared for their task, being well-instructed in the doctrine

of the church and possessing both a pastoral and theoretical knowledge of the laws of psychology and of educational methods. (14)

Each pastor shares in this duty by ensuring that parish catechists have adequate preparation and continuing formation for their ministry.

Many dioceses provide substantial regional training and formation programs for catechists, which might otherwise be difficult to provide at every parish. These programs and diocesan services should be supported and challenged to deliver excellent professional training.

Catechists must see to it that prayer is an integral part of the plan of catechesis and formation. Catechists also may be called on to lead catechumens and candidates in prayer, and so should be given the training to do so. With the bishop's mandate, catechists may preside at the minor exorcisms and blessings contained in the ritual (16).

Bishops

As the chief shepherds of the local church, bishops are the overseers of the Christian initiation process.

> Bishops are the chief stewards of the mysteries of God and leaders of the entire liturgical life in the church committed to them. They thus direct the conferring of baptism, by which a sharing in the kingly priesthood of Christ is granted. Therefore they should personally celebrate baptism, especially at the Easter Vigil. The preparation and baptism of adults is entrusted to them in a special way. (*Christian Initiation*, General Introduction, 12)

The *Rite of Christian Initiation of Adults* gives a more specific description of the bishop's duties regarding the process of initiation:

> The bishop, in person or through his delegate, sets up, regulates and promotes the pastoral formation of catechumens and admits the candidates to their election and to the sacraments. It is hoped that, presiding if possible at the lenten liturgy, he will himself celebrate the rite of election and, at the Easter Vigil, the sacraments of initiation, at least for the initiation of those fourteen years old or older. Finally, when pastoral care requires, the bishop should depute catechists, truly worthy and properly prepared, to celebrate the minor exorcism and the blessings of the catechumens. (12)

The bishop's leadership is important to preserve the order of initiation from becoming isolated from the larger church. His role is not to set up inflexible standards or to develop identical programs for every community but to assure active catechumenates in each area of the diocese and to maintain strong bonds between the catechumens and candidates and the diocesan church.

In celebrating the Rite of Election at the beginning of Lent, the bishop exercises an important pastoral role (121). Within the Rite of Election the bishop declares in the presence of the community the church's approval of the catechumens (122), which is founded on the election by God, in whose name the church acts (119). The bishop's involvement in the Rite of Election manifests his role as pastor, teacher, preacher, evangelizer, shepherd and priest of the local church.

In preparation for the Rite of Rlection, the bishop might meet with catechumens and candidates in the course of his pastoral visits throughout the diocese. Listening to their concerns and questions and sharing his own perspective on the church and its faith can be beneficial to the catechumens and candidates and to the bishop himself. On these visits he might also preside over presentations of the Creed or the Lord's Prayer or one of the scrutinies and exorcisms.

The *Rite of Christian Initiation of Adults* notes that the bishop can show his pastoral concern for the new members of the church by meeting the recently initiated at least once in the year and presiding at the celebration of the eucharist with them (251). In some dioceses it has become a custom for the bishop to celebrate a Mass of thanksgiving with the newly initiated during the Easter Season.

Priests

> Priests, in addition to their usual ministry for any celebration of baptism, confirmation and eucharist, have the responsibility of attending to the pastoral and personal care of the catechumens, especially those who are hesitant and discouraged. With the help of deacons and catechists, they are to provide instruction for the catechumens; they are also to approve the choice of godparents and willingly listen to and help them; they are to be diligent in the correct celebration and adaptation of the rites throughout the whole course of Christian initiation. (13)

The primary role of the priest in the initiation process is to serve as the overseer of the process in the parish. He sees to it that the vision and process of initiation is woven into the fabric of parish life. He is to take particular care in ministering to the initiation team, offering them support and encouragement, providing for their formation and listening to their needs and experiences.

While the priest is a steward of God's word and the church's teachings, he exercises his responsibility for catechesis with others who have been prepared for this ministry. Not to share this responsibility could result in giving the unfortunate impression to catechumens and candidates that the laity are not capable of communicating the faith or not expected to do so.

One of the most important roles entrusted to the priest is to preside at the various rites of initiation. As the preacher on these occasions, the priest must be well acquainted with the catechumens and candidates. He needs to know something of their backgrounds and of their hopes, fears and doubts so that he can preach the word of God effectively to them and to the community that gathers with them.

Although the parish priest should take a great interest in the church's order of initiation, it would be shortsighted of him to assume total responsibility for the initiation process. The vision of the church's way of initiating new Catholics demands that leaders from the community are an integral and active part of the process. This helps assure that Christian initiation is anchored in parish life and not dependent on the assignment of pastors.

For many priests, convert instructions of the past were a very satisfying part of priestly ministry. The individual, personal contact with adults over matters of spiritual depth and meaning left many priests with pastoral experiences they have valued and always remembered. Sharing the ministry of initiation should not deprive the priest of these treasured opportunities. On the contrary, the church looks to the parish priest to be available for pastoral counsel to catechumens and candidates as well as to sponsors, godparents, catechists and others who may be sharing in the outreach to future Catholics.

Deacons

Deacons are closely associated with priests in the ministry of initiation (13, 15). They may preside at some of the initiation rites and preach. In those areas where priests are not available, the deacon may be expected to assume some of the responsibilities ordinarily assigned to the parish priest.

Permanent deacons especially may be well suited for introducing candidates and catechumens to works of charity and justice. A deacon also may serve as one of the catechists if he has been trained in adult catechesis.

In general, the deacon's involvement will depend on local need and on his own gifts. Ordinarily, however, a deacon should not act as sponsor or godparent. Rather, his ministry to those being initiated should be focused more broadly.

Liturgists and Musicians

Because the liturgy is so integral to the order of initiation, liturgists and musicians must be interested and involved in the parish's initiation ministry. Rites that will take place at the Sunday assembly should be planned with the assistance of the liturgists and musicians so that the rites are integrated into the overall liturgical life of the community. If the liturgical rites are poorly prepared, their meaning and significance may be diminished. A weak, unconnected rite will seem to be an interruption of the liturgy and so may annoy the congregation rather than involve them in this important aspect of the church's life.

Because music is such an integral part of the liturgy, musicians should work closely with catechists to introduce music into the catechumens' and candidates' formation. Liturgical musicians can help catechumens and candidates discover spiritual and theological teaching contained in the musical texts and can help to prepare them for active and conscious participation in the liturgy.

Spiritual Directors or Companions

In many ways the entire process of Christian initiation is a type of spiritual direction. Pastors and catechumenal leaders have the awesome responsibility of being catalysts for spiritual growth. Through liturgical rites, spontaneous prayer, instruction, dialogue and group activities, men and women are introduced into a Christian way of life and encouraged to develop their own vision of life and self that reflects the way of Jesus and the tradition of the church.

While the potential for spiritual direction through participation in the catechumenal community should not be underestimated, one-on-one spiritual direction is also valuable. Individual spiritual direction allows a person the opportunity to focus on his or her own life and gifts to develop a personal response to the Christian mystery.

What is spiritual direction? The definition offered by Katherine Dyckman and L. Patrick Carroll is helpful:

> Spiritual direction [is] an interpersonal relationship in which one person assists others to reflect on their own experience in the light of who they are called to become in fidelity to the gospel. *(Inviting the Mystic, Supporting the Prophet* [New York: Paulist Press, 1981])

Spiritual direction helps people discern what God wants of them in light of the gospel. The spiritual director does not tell one what to do or how to do it, but rather assists one to recognize the voice of God in his or her own life. The spiritual director is a mentor, a companion, a facilitator. A good spiritual director recognizes the need to listen to the Spirit in his or her own life. He or she knows the struggle of faith and prayer and is a good listener.

Who can serve as spiritual director, companion or guide? The ministry of spiritual direction is not reserved to clergy or religious. Whoever is chosen ought to receive some training, but that person must first be a faithful and stable person. Those chosen for this ministry should meet regularly with their own spiritual directors.

The spiritual companion or director need not be a regular participant in the catechumenate sessions. It may be preferable if they were not part of the catechumenate team that assesses whether the candidate is ready for the initiation sacraments. Spiritual directors do not judge those whom they direct, nor are they free to divulge the content of their conversations.

Catechumens and candidates are not obliged to choose a spiritual director, but they should know who is available in that role to assist them.

Hospitality

The ministry of hospitality can set the tone for the entire initiation process. Opening doors, arranging the room, setting out coffee and cookies, welcoming people as they arrive — these simple actions let people know they are welcome and cared about, and this is the heart of Christian initiation. Responsibility for hospitality could be shared among the organizations of the parish or any parishioners who are interested in doing their part in the initiation of new members and who have a gift for friendliness.

Ministries — A Postscript

The long list of ministries noted in this chapter (and others that still could be added) may leave one with the impression that initiation is a very complex network of ministries and sophisticated structures. This need not be so.

In smaller parishes, especially in rural areas, there may be a feeling of frustration because the number of personnel available to minister may be few. But smaller parishes often have the advantage of being close-knit communities where the parish itself is truly the catechumenal community. The mark of an effective catechumenate is not the number of different ministries that can be created or how intricate or how complex a plan can be developed. Rather, the ultimate test is whether the inquirers, catechumens and candidates, elect and newly initiated are experiencing a genuine welcome and absorbing the Catholic way of life from enough people to catch a fair and complete picture of the Catholic church.

Large city and suburban parishes often must develop complex structures only because the size of the parish and the number of catechumens and candidates demands an order to what might otherwise be a widely dispensed congregation. Rural communities and smaller city parishes need not try to model their pastoral plan on the large-parish paradigm. Smaller communities have strengths upon which they should build their own structure and network of ministries.

CHAPTER FIVE

Pastoral Questions

and Issues

■ **Are there many inquirers today?**

Many people are searching for religious values to help them set a direction and find meaning for their lives. The Gallup Study, "The Unchurched American" (1988), reported that 44 percent of the U.S. population do not belong to a church or synagogue, or have not attended services in the last six months. At the same time, 66 percent indicated that God was important to them, a 6 percent increase since a 1978 finding.

This means that the work of evangelization complements the work of initiation. There are people interested in pursuing their religious questions and open to the experience of a Christian community. But we must invite them. Pastors know well the answer converts have often given when asked why they had not joined the church before: "No one ever asked me."

Members of Catholic assemblies must discover their vocation as evangelizers. They are the ones who meet the unchurched at work or over the backyard fence. Their words and witness will attract and encourage a prospective inquirer to take the first step in the journey of conversion and church membership.

Evangelization efforts are not just a matter of programs to attract newcomers. Evangelization is most effective in a parish that is responding to the needs of people. Word spreads when a parish has something to offer through its people and their worship, ministries and programs. A reputation for faith, service and fellowship attracts others and is the best evangelization program.

■ What happens when someone is planning to marry soon and would like to be initiated before the wedding?

Christian marriage is a serious vocation. Anyone planning to marry should prepare carefully for marriage. It is far better to obtain a dispensation for a Catholic/non-Catholic marriage and postpone the catechumenate process until after the wedding than to rush through the preparations for initiation while preparing for marriage. Becoming a Catholic for the convenience of the wedding would seldom allow the time required by the very nature of the initiation process. If the non-Catholic party is genuinely interested in becoming a Catholic, then he or she can enter the catechumenate after the wedding.

There are exceptions, of course. Occasionally, someone may need very little formation before initiation; special arrangements for a shorter period of preparation may be made even when there is no impending marriage. The *Rite of Christian Initiation of Adults* sees initiation not as an obstacle course but as pastoral care for each individual, and so it is flexible. This flexibility should not become an excuse for the convenient sacrificing of the integrity of the initiation process.

■ Can we initiate someone when there is a canonical marriage impediment involved?

Anyone who is being initiated into the church must be free to celebrate the sacraments. Very early in the initiation process the marital status of the inquirer should be ascertained through a personal interview. If an annulment is required by the church, that process should begin immediately. Participation in the catechumenate is not recommended until the marriage situation is resolved. Otherwise the individual becomes attached to the catechumenate community and begins to expect to be initiated at the next Easter, only to discover that initiation cannot take place then. Support for the inquirer through spiritual direction and sponsorship is a better solution. Once the marriage status has been resolved as far as church law requires, the individual is free to proceed through the complete process of initiation.

If a community judges that it is pastorally advantageous to include men and women whose marital status has yet to be resolved, those men and women may participate in the catechumenate up to the rite of election.

■ Is the Easter Vigil the only time the sacraments of initiation may be celebrated?

From very early times the church has seen Easter as a most appropriate time for Christian initiation, for it is through the sacraments of initiation that

> men and women are freed from the power of darkness. With Christ they die, are buried, and rise again. They receive the Spirit of adoption that makes them God's sons and daughters and with the entire people of God they celebrate the memorial of the Lord's death and resurrection. (*Christian Initiation*, General Introduction, 1)

When it is necessary to initiate new members outside the Easter Vigil (perhaps because their formation could not be completed by then), a date during the Easter Season (such as the Solemnity of Pentecost) is preferred because of the closeness of the nature of initiation to the death and rising of Jesus. Even a date outside the Easter Season should carry the meaning of that season.

■ When should one celebrate the sacrament of penance?

Those who are preparing for baptism do not celebrate the sacrament of penance before they are initiated. Catechumens should, however, be catechized about the sacrament of penance and be encouraged to celebrate the sacrament in the future.

For candidates preparing to be received into full communion, the most suitable time to celebrate this sacrament would be during Lent. This rite can be significant as the penitents turn firmly from whatever sinfulness they remember from their past. Pastors should assist each individual in determining the right moment.

The support of sponsors may be helpful to the candidates as they celebrate this sacrament for the first time. They may wish to accompany them to the church and, perhaps, prepare for the sacrament together. Because many non-Catholics often have been given a poor impression of reconciliation (often by Catholics), it is important for the sponsor to approach this sacrament thoughtfully and with joy.

The general norms for reconciliation apply to the baptized candidates: No one can be obliged to celebrate the sacrament of reconciliation except for serious sin (482). If they have been catechized well and have had the opportunity to resolve their fears or misunderstandings, most candidates will want to celebrate the sacrament.

■ If Christians being received into the full communion of the Catholic church have already been confirmed in another denomination, do we confirm them again?

The Catholic church confirms baptized Christians when they are received into full communion. While many Christian churches celebrate the presence of the Holy Spirit in the person who is maturing, Roman Catholics believe that confirmation is one of the seven sacraments instituted by Christ for the church. With baptism and eucharist, the sacrament of confirmation is necessary to be fully initiated into the Catholic church.

■ Does this apply to those who are entering the Roman Catholic church from the Orthodox church?

No. Orthodox Christians share the same seven sacraments as Roman Catholics. An Orthodox Christian who has been confirmed (called "chrismation" in Orthodox churches) enters into the Catholic church by making a profession of faith.

■ What if new inquirers approach the parish long after the precatechumenate has begun?

The Holy Spirit may lead people to our doors at any time of the year. Regardless of the time, they should be warmly welcomed. After a personal interview, they may join the precatechumenate group. Because the agenda for the precatechumenate is shaped by the needs of the inquirers, there should be little difficulty integrating the new inquirer into the group.

Ideally the precatechumenate will be available all year long. Perhaps a family or group of individuals can take responsibility for a weekly open-door precatechumenate. When individuals are ready to move on to the catechumenate, they simply join the catechumenate group whenever it meets. The catechumenate group also would meet year-round, presumably after being dismissed after Sunday's liturgy of the word.

■ Can a college campus be the setting for a catechumenal process?

The college years often are a time for conversion. As the students' world expands and they begin to look inward, they frequently ask important questions about life's purpose and meaning. They look to the future and seek hope and direction.

Where there is an active Newman Center or Catholic presence on campus, college students may discover that the church has a great deal to offer them. Some may not have been raised in a religious environment. Others may have a religious background but until now never paid much attention to it.

Some college-centered catechumenate groups encounter difficulty when the school year calendar is out of sync with the liturgical year calendar. The initiation process is intended to culminate at the Easter Vigil, but at many schools the Triduum coincides with spring break. In these instances the sacraments of initiation may best be celebrated on the Second or Third Sunday of Easter or on the Solemnity of Pentecost. The initiation sacraments would not be celebrated during Lent.

Other pastoral concerns that arise for a campus-centered catechumenal process are the period of mystagogy and integration into a parish community. Catechumenal teams will need to develop a support system for the newly initiated that can continue beyond campus life. Guidance in choosing a sponsor who will be able to maintain contact would be wise. Communication with pastors where the newly initiated make their home will help provide a supportive link.

What if someone's psychological or emotional needs are greater than the catechumenal process can fulfill?

It is not uncommon that individuals searching for psychological or emotional wholeness will look in many directions for peace of mind. Often they eventually look to religion for the answer to their problems or anxieties.

While we believe that religious faith does help us to live a peaceful and integrated life, sometimes the psychological needs overpower all else and must be addressed professionally before participation in a catechumenal community is advised. The catechumenal community is not a therapy group, but rather presumes the participation of mature and healthy adults.

Interviews prior to participation in the catechumenal group will be very important for surfacing any serious psychological or emotional problems. When these problems arise in the interviews or in the group, the individual should be encouraged to seek professional help. Even though he or she may not be taken immediately into the catechumenal community, the pastoral team still can maintain a pastoral relationship and keep close contact with the individual. This situation requires great sensitivity. Parish teams should discuss the possibility of such a situation arising and how they will address it.

■ Can we use the *Rite of Christian Initiation of Adults* as a renewal program for Catholics?

Christian communities need to be committed to ongoing renewal. However, the *Rite of Christian Initiation of Adults* is reserved for those who are preparing for the sacraments of initiation. If the rite is used for everyone, its impact and its unique character may be diluted.

Nevertheless, there is much we can learn from the *Rite of Christian Initiation of Adults* that can be applied in caring for the spiritual renewal of a community. In particular, the dynamics of evangelization, conversion, sponsorship, ritual prayer and apostolic involvement may give shape to a parish's renewal efforts. Whether in small groups or as a larger group process, parishioners can be led through a process of spiritual formation that is distinct from the catechumens but inspired by the same dynamics.

We should also note that when a community walks through the liturgical year with catechumens and candidates and observes Lent, the Triduum and Easter in all their fullness, the community will experience a genuine spirit of renewal.

Glossary

Baptismal font. A large vessel that holds the water used in the baptism of infants and adults, either by immersion or infusion (pouring). The baptismal font usually is located in a place that allows for full congregational participation.

Candidate. Generally, anyone preparing to become a Catholic, but the term often is used to denote a person baptized in another Christian tradition who is preparing for reception into the full communion of the Roman Catholic church.

Canon law. The body of law that governs church practice and protects the rights and privileges of individuals and of the community.

Catechesis. The instruction and spiritual formation of catechumens, neophytes and those persons who seek full communion with the Catholic church.

Catechumen. An unbaptized person who is seeking initiation into the church and who has been accepted into the order of catechumens.

Catechumenate. The process by which the Catholic church brings unbaptized children and adults to Christian initiation.

Chrism. A combination of oil and sweet balsam or perfume that is mixed and consecrated by the bishop, and used to anoint newly baptized people and newly ordained priests and bishops. Chrism also is used in the consecration of churches and altars.

Doctrine. The formal teachings of the church.

Elect. A catechumen who has been found ready by the community of faith to take part in the next celebration of the sacraments of initiation.

Election. The process of selecting those catechumens who are considered ready to take part in the next celebration of the sacraments of initiation; the celebration ordinarily takes place on the First Sunday of Lent, wherein the bishop or his delegate declares in the name of the church that particular catechumens are ready and chosen for the sacraments at Easter. During this celebration, the names of the elect are written in the Book of the Elect.

Enlightenment. The period of Lent during which the elect are involved in the final stage of preparation for celebrating the rites of initiation. *Synonyms:* illumination, purification.

Enrollment. The rite of inscribing into the Book of the Elect the names of those catechumens elected to take part in the next celebration of the sacraments of initiation. *See* election.

Ephphetha. An optional rite in which the presider touches the ears and the mouth of the elect and prays that they be open to hear and proclaim the word of God in faith. It may be celebrated as part of the preparation rites on Holy Saturday.

Evangelization. The activity by which the church proclaims the gospel in word or in deed.

Exorcisms. Prayers for the deliverance from the powers of evil and falsehood, and for the reception of the gifts of the Lord, especially the Spirit. Exorcisms are part of the rites of scrutiny.

Fasting. A form of sacrifice by which faithful Christians join themselves with the suffering and death of Jesus by forgoing food for a specific period of time. On Ash Wednesday and on Good Friday, Catholics who are in good health and between the ages of 18 and 59 (inclusive) are obliged to fast in a modified way: One full meal and two other small meals may be eaten, and no food is eaten between meals. Catholics are encouraged to keep a paschal fast from Holy Thursday evening until after the Easter Vigil in anticipation of the celebration of the Lord's resurrection.

Godparent. The person who accompanies the catechumen during the rites and periods of election, initiation and mystagogy. This person (or persons) is selected by the catechumen with the approval of the pastor and, if possible, of the local parish.

Illumination. *See* enlightenment.

Immersion. A way of baptizing in which the person is partially or entirely submerged in the baptismal water.

Infusion. A way of baptizing in which water is poured over the head of the person.

Initiation. The process by which a person enters the faith life of the church. The process extends from the person's first inquiry through the completion of mystagogy.

Inquirers. Persons who sincerely seek to learn about the faith of the church.

Lectionary. A book containing the assigned scripture readings for the celebration of the eucharist and the other sacraments.

Lectionary-based catechesis. A catechetical method for learning the foundation of faith and doctrine by study of and reflection on the scriptures as they are arranged for the liturgy over a three-year cycle.

Liturgy of the hours. A form of prayer consisting of scriptural prayers, songs and readings for morning, daytime, evening and nighttime of each feast, season, Sunday and weekday.

Magisterium. The official teaching office of the church as it is exercised by the pope in communion with all the bishops of the church.

Mystagogy. The period of time following initiation, usually the Easter Season, which centers on catechesis in the meaning and experience of the mysteries of baptismal faith.

Neophyte. A newly baptized person who is in the final period of Christian initiation, mystagogy.

Oil of catechumens. The blessed oil used in anointing catechumens as a sign of their need for and God's offer of strength in overcoming all opposition to the faith they will profess throughout their life.

Order of Christian initiation. The progression of catechesis and rituals that make up the process of bringing a person to faith in Christ and membership in the church. The term sometimes refers to the text used for initiation, *Rite of Christian Initiation of Adults.*

Paschal candle. The large candle lighted each year from the new fire ignited and blessed at the Easter Vigil. From this light, representing the risen Lord who destroys the darkness of sin, the newly baptized light their candles.

Paschal Triduum. The three days from Holy Thursday evening through Easter Sunday that celebrate the passover of Israel from slavery to freedom, the passover of Jesus Christ from death to life, our own passover from sin to grace and the world's passover from darkness to light.

Periods. Times of growth in the Christian initiation process: 1) inquiry, or precatechumenate; 2) catechumenate; 3) purification and enlightenment; 4) mystagogy.

Postbaptismal. After baptism.

Precatechumenate. The period of inquiry prior to acceptance into the order of catechumens; the time of initial evangelization.

Presentations. The rites during the period of purification and enlightenment through which the church passes on to the elect the Creed and the Lord's Prayer, the most cherished documents of the church, and the traditions they represent: the way Christians believe and the way Christians pray.

Purification. *See* enlightenment.

Reconciliation room. A place for the celebration of the sacrament of penance. A reconciliation room is set up so that penitents may either meet face-to-face with the priest or confess anonymously from behind a screen. These rooms are sometimes called reconciliation chapels or confessionals.

Sacramentary. The book that contains the prayers spoken or sung by the presider at the eucharistic celebration.

Scrutinies. Rites celebrated with the elect, usually at the Sunday liturgy on the Third, Fourth and Fifth Sundays of Lent, petitioning for the spirit of repentance, an understanding of sin and the experience of the true freedom of the children of God.

Sponsors. Those persons who accompany the inquirers when they seek acceptance into the order of catechumens and who remain with them as companions during the catechumenate until the Rite of Election.